£1

GW01445321

GOOD KING WENCESLAS

GOOD KING WENCESLAS

A CAROL WRITTEN BY DR. NEALE · PICTURES BY ARTHUR GASKIN · WITH AN INTRODUCTION BY WILLIAM MORRIS

HINGHAM · MASSACHUSETTS
M · CM · IV

INTRODUCTORY NOTE

THE POEM HERE illustrated by Mr. Gaskin's beautiful pictures was written to suit a Mediæval tune by Dr. John Mason Neale, who was one of the leaders in the early days of the Ritualistic movement. Dr. Neale was a representative of a side of the movement, which, unless I am mistaken has almost died out as a special characteristic of Ritualism—the historical side to wit. This has happened I think because of the growth amongst thinking people generally of a sense of the importance of Mediæval history, and of the increasing knowledge that the ecclesiastical part of it cannot be dissociated from its civil & popular parts. Mediæval history in all its detail, with all its enthusiasms, legends, and superstitions, is now cultivated by many who have no ecclesiastical bias as a portion of the great progress of the life of man on the earth, the discovery of which as an unbroken chain belongs almost entirely to our own days. But to Dr. Neale must be awarded the honour of being the chief figure of the history lovers, or shall we say the Mediævalists in the movement in question, and the poem before us is a good specimen of his manner & its limitations. The legend itself is pleasing and a genuine one, and the Christmas-like quality of it, recalling the times of my boyhood, appeals to me at least as a happy memory of past days.

As this preface is a part of the book and not a criticism of it as a work of art I must not say much of the merits of the pictures done by my friend Mr. Gaskin; but I cannot help saying that

b

they have given me very much pleasure, both as achievements in themselves and as giving hopes of a turn towards the ornamental side of illustration, which is most desirable.

WILLIAM MORRIS.

September 1894.

GOOD KING WENCESLAS

GOOD KING WENCESLAS

GOOD KING WENCESLAS
LOOK'D OUT
ON THE FEAST OF
STEPHEN,
WHEN THE SNOW LAY
ROUND ABOUT,
DEEP, AND CRISP, AND EVEN.
BRIGHTLY SHONE THE
MOON THAT NIGHT,
THOUGH THE FROST
WAS CRUEL,
WHEN A POOR MAN CAME
IN SIGHT
GATH'RING WINTER FUEL.

HITHER, PAGE & STAND BY ME
IF THOU KNOW'ST IT,
TELLING,
YONDER PEASANT,
WHO IS HE?
WHERE, AND WHAT
HIS DWELLING?"
"SIRE, HE LIVES A GOOD
LEAGUE HENCE,
UNDERNEATH THE
MOUNTAIN:
RIGHT AGAINST THE
FOREST FENCE,
BY SAINT AGNES' FOUNTAIN."

BRING ME FLESH, AND
BRING ME WINE,
BRING ME PINE-LOGS
HITHER:
THOU AND I WILL SEE
HIM DINE
WHEN WE BEAR THEM
THITHER."
PAGE AND MONARCH,
FORTH THEY WENT,
FORTH THEY WENT
TOGETHER;
THROUGH THE RUDE
WINDS LOUD LAMENT
AND THE BITTER WEATHER.

SIRE THE NIGHT IS
DARKER NOW,
AND THE WIND BLOWS
STRONGER;
FAILS MY HEART, I KNOW
NOT HOW.
I CAN GO NO LONGER."
"MARK MY FOOTSTEPS,
MY GOOD PAGE,
TREAD THOU IN THEM
BOLDLY;
THOU SHALT FIND THE
WINTER WIND
FREEZE THY BLOOD
LESS COLDLY."

IN HIS MASTER'S STEPS
HE TROD,
WHERE THE SNOW LAY
DINTED;
HEAT WAS IN THE VERY SOD
WHICH THE SAINT
HAD PRINTED.
THEREFORE, CHRISTIAN
MEN, BE SURE
WEALTH OR RANK
POSSESSING,
YE WHO NOW WILL BLESS
THE POOR,
SHALL YOURSELVES
FIND BLESSING.

Reprinted from the edition issued by
Cornish Brothers. Double border and
title from drawings by Will Dwig‑
gins. One hundred eighty‑five copies
printed by hand at the Village Press,
Hingham, Massachusetts, by Fred &
Bertha Goudy, and finished the 19th
day of November, 1904.

The Village Press

Fred W Goudy
Bertha Goudy

Lightning Source UK Ltd.
Milton Keynes UK
UKHW022024091221
395394UK00006B/1435